mementos

mementos
seasons in verse

inga e.b.

Columbus, Ohio

This book is a work of fiction. The names, characters and events in this book are the products of the author's imagination or are used fictitiously. Any similarity to real persons living or dead is coincidental and not intended by the author.

The views and opinions expressed in this book are solely those of the author and do not reflect the views or opinions of Gatekeeper Press. Gatekeeper Press is not to be held responsible for and expressly disclaims responsibility of the content herein.

mementos: seasons in verse

Published by Gatekeeper Press
2167 Stringtown Rd, Suite 109
Columbus, OH 43123-2989
www.GatekeeperPress.com

Copyright © 2021 by Inga Buccella
All rights reserved. Neither this book, nor any parts within it may be sold or reproduced in any form or by any electronic or mechanical means, including information storage and retrieval systems, without permission in writing from the author. The only exception is by a reviewer, who may quote short excerpts in a review.

ISBN (hardcover): 9781662913518

I have known Inga since high school. In our little group, she was always the "artistic one." I could only dream of being able to draw and create as she did. Fast forward a few years and we find ourselves on the other side of loss, maybe not together but at the same time. Parents, siblings, spouses. The only constant is perhaps how personal each loss is. Personal and, at the same time, mutable. The shimmering something that catches your eye while you're looking away, thinking about something else, and then you see it and remember. We know the presence of absence.

In *memento*, Inga has conjured up the exact essence of that liminal space between what we have left and what will be left. Tangy words make sharp strikes then retreat, leaving us to wonder, *How am I different now?* Having her own set of grief credentials, Inga makes meaning of the unknowable with images intertwined to memory and, ultimately, hope. As in her novella, *In the Age of Buoyancy*, and her children's book, *Forever Feathers*, Inga holds out her open hand to both grief and life.

In these days of uncertainty and daily change to habits and patterns, we need a way into that place without steady walls. Where we can imagine a new sound, a new smell, a different kind of weather and be with it, knowing that all life is change. And, knowing also, a memento is there when we need a reminder.

Michelle Pauls
Actor/Writer
4/2021

me*men*to

1. Something that serves as a reminder of what is past or gone; keepsake; souvenir.
2. Anything serving as a reminder or warning.
3. Either of two prayers in the canon of the Roman Catholic Mass, one for persons living and the other for persons dead.

table of contents

winter 1
   january at the museum. 2
   the collection. 3
   ethology 4
   botany in winter 5

spring. 7
   dancer 8
   new artifact 9
   land line 10
   mid life. 11

summer. 13
   the timelessness of a comet. 14
   children's games 16
   buoyancy. 17

fall 19
   visit 20
   on making a prism 21
   loose ends 22
   the way. 23

novus. 25
   april at the museum 26

winter

january at the museum

we walked into the dali painting
amongst the looming heads
filled with air
not stone
maybe from an island

we three
connected by you
without you
this time
on an island
faces on brick
nestled in the snow

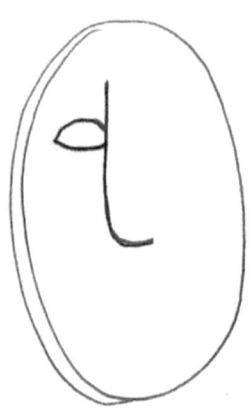

the collection

musty boxes
of unearthed stamps
clinging to
yellow cellophane
envelope skins
foreign addresses
posted in cobalt

dusty muses
dance on brass and silver
greek and japanese coins
all circular
some with punched-out centers
tokens
of the well-lived life

brittle glossies
rippled white edges of
family fragments
smiles and squints
in front of
black shrubbery
scenery

ethology

white and austere
and at first arid
with a metallic aftertaste

no one is prepared for
its noisy void
its chronic voice

but it waits for us all
heaving gray clouds
of perilous vapors

botany in winter

when the frozen blanket is thick
and you cannot see the grass
when the end of his life
is too hard to grasp

when the days are short
but the season is long
and the minutes pass like hours
sung like a mournful song

one sunrise you will hear
a young robin's voice
it is then that you will have to
make a pinnacle choice

will you now feel like an orphan?
perhaps you have not known
throughout the entire journey
the seeds that *you* have sown

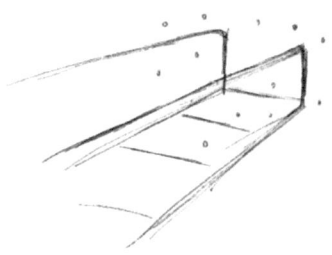

inga e.b

spring

dancer

an element
no, more like a star
who finally
came to be

a girl,
yes — but even more
for in her eyes
the roar of the sea

her laugh
her grace, her way
and her mind
all now intertwined

her dance
though brief, was so refined
the soft steps she left behind
forever etched in time

new artifact

ire at the entity
indignation
towards a deity

mere words on tape
rarely cement together

the distance between
finite
and
forever
but we have discovered
a tether to bind us together

buried in a deep-rooted tree
and called it
your story

land line

between heaven and earth
are dreams
made from memories
of you and me

mid life

did we
have
the fortune
or curse
of
seeing
your
entire
beautiful existence
begin, but then
end,
in
the
middle
of
ours?

inga e.b

summer

the timelessness of a comet

brilliance beyond
shining too bright
just a glimpse of the star
can harm your eyesight

growing for eons
this powerful beam will transcend
in fact, it is probable
it may never end

tho his life here with you
may seem concluded
you will gaze skyward one night
realizing that clouds have not muted

a sight you have never seen
blazing through an ebony curtain
spanning centuries of time
of this you will be certain

his time here on earth
seemed too brief to understand
but like the light of his smile
a shooting star that will never land

children's games

in follow the leader
you were mine

you were two years ahead
i was two behind

in red light green light
you were the light, pacing me

now I'm older than you were
when you were set free

while playing hide and seek
you would find me under the sink

as babies, I was dressed in blue
you were dressed in pink

i'm not used to being
the leader or pacing myself

and I will never stop searching
for you
and me
and not just that picture on a shelf

buoyancy

on a wing

or a wave

a plummeting bird

or

a sinking ship

that's saved

flying, not falling

it's a siren calling

the longing comes later

a song sung

from future's daughter

floating on air

buoyed by sea

on a wing

or on a wave

it's who we dare

be

fall

visit

sitting at the kitchen table, bathed in autumn light while in the midst of a sentence, i wasn't the first to notice her. spinning round, she was behind me, outside in the garden. i was startled by her dignified presence, and the splendor of both her size and color. perched on the wrought iron gate, not even ten feet away — but with glass between us, she surveyed.

she reminded me of a tall, russet-haired woman i once knew, with stately features and a strong posture. but this regal creature before me had feathers, not hair; and stealth talons, for stability and survival.

for a lifetime we stood — frozen in admiration, tinged with awe. i watched and waited, as she watched and waited, with one unblinking eye, like her silver silhouetted cousin.

then the young female floated back up to her home in the heavens. but not before the red-tailed hawk had glared deep onto our eyes and captured every one of our souls.

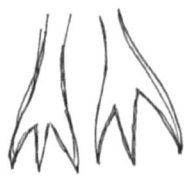

on making a prism

it's rain falling thru sun rays
or a death coinciding with a birth

it's sporadic sadness
but then it's the moments of mirth

unpredictable weather sometimes
causes frozen white-hot earth

don't ask why I'm sad
it's a complicated truth

it stings my eyes when the tears fall
that's how it starts at first

it's the best of times for sure
but somehow also the desolate worst

so let me rise to the occasions
while preparing for the fall

still searching for a promise
of tomorrow's rainbow waterfall

loose ends

the void was vast and deep
three evergreens in the yard
still dance, but weep

if you told me back when the leaves fell
that a year later it would all go to hell
it would not have made a difference this time
because you
are still
indelible
in my heart and mind

piano and pooh try to say their goodbyes
how many more times do we need to try?

limbs have lost their memory to hug
but certain talons continue to tug
…for now
loose ends

the way

time is not enough
of anything to bring me
the source of peace that is
currently required

but the sun and moon
and the planets in their entirety
are enough to lead me
the rest of the way

novus

april at the museum

crushed wild grass blades
flower buds bursting with pink
overtaking the symmetry of
the labyrinth on the hill
not overshadowing
its importance
but humbly ushering us
into the masonry structure

sporadic murmurings
echoes of heels-clicking
cascading sepia tones
on a red wall
black and white photos
of racial injustice
pandemic moments
behind glass

winter is finally
frozen
your absence is still
heavy
but spring's breath is now
light
at my library of art
sunday morning at the museum

by inga
eissmann
buccella

with daily rituals of drawing and writing, nature in all forms, is Inga's muse.

poetry is both a voice and vice for inga. her lyrical style can be heard throughout all of her poems and stories.

animals, especially her small dog, agusto, are her favorite subjects to draw. she has created custom pet and people illustrations for many years. you can see examples of her work at her etsy shop, pupspressions.

inga resides with her husband, dog, and 29-year-old water frog named prima, in southeastern pennsylvania.

www.ingramcontent.com/pod-product-compliance
Lightning Source LLC
LaVergne TN
LVHW042004060526
838200LV00041B/1878